INVISIBLE WORLDS

Inside Plants

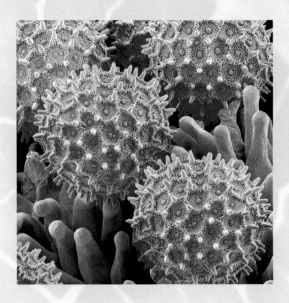

Barbara Taylor

Marshall Cavendish
Benchmark
New York

Other Marshall Cavendish Offices:
Marshall Cavendish International (Asia) Private Limited, 1 New Industrial Road, Singapore 536196 • Marshall Cavendish International (Thailand)
Co Ltd. 253 Asoke, 12th Flr, Sukhumvit 21 Road, Klongtoey Nua, Wattana, Bangkok 10110, Thailand • Marshall Cavendish (Malaysia) Sdn Bhd,
Times Subang, Lot 46, Subang Hi-Tech Industrial Park, Batu Tiga, 40000 Shah Alam, Selangor Darul Ehsan, Malaysia

Marshall Cavendish is a trademark of Times Publishing Limited

All websites were available and accurate when this book was sent to press.

Library of Congress Cataloging-in-Publication Data
Taylor, Barbara, 1954–
Inside plants / by Barbara Taylor.
p. cm. — (Invisible worlds)
"Describes the fascinating plant details that are too small for the unaided eye to see,
and how these microscopic systems work to keep the plant alive and healthy"—Provided by publisher.
Includes bibliographical references and index.
ISBN 978-0-7614-4189-2
1. Plants—Juvenile literature. I. Title.
QK49.T38 2010
580—dc22   2008037247

Series created by The Brown Reference Group
www.brownreference.com

For The Brown Reference Group:
Editor: Leon Gray
Designer: Joan Curtis
Picture Managers: Sophie Mortimer and Clare Newman
Picture Researcher: Sean Hannaway
Illustrator: MW Digital Graphics
Managing Editor: Miranda Smith
Design Manager: David Poole
Editorial Director: Lindsey Lowe
Children's Publisher: Anne O'Daly

Consultant: Dr. Nicholas Turland

Front cover: Science Photo Library/Eye of Science; inset: Alamy/Jeremy Pardoe

The photographs in this book are used by permission and through the courtesy of:
Science Photo Library: Biology Media 37; Biophoto Associates 21, 22–23; Dr. Jeremy Burgess 4–5, 7, 8, 36, 44; Eye of Science 19 (top), 30 (top);
Gilbert Grant 34: Steve Gschmeissner 14, 16, 25, 28; Susumu Nishinaga 1, 27, 33, 39, 42 (top); J .C. Revt 24; Sinclair Stammers 23 (top); M. I.
Walker 10, 13; Jim Zipp 40: Shutterstock: Tilly Parizia 34 (bottom); Anna Dzonazua 11.

Contents

Introducing Plants

Plants are different from other living things. Animals eat plants or other animals to get their energy. Plants make their own food using energy from the Sun. Plants do not see or hear by using eyes and ears. And plants keep growing all through their lives.

Plants are some of the oldest and tallest living things. Some trees are thousands of years old. The tallest coast redwood trees of California are taller than the Statue of Liberty (305 feet or 93 meters).

No one knows how many different kinds, or species, of plants live on Earth. There could be more than 400,000. There were plants long before animals appeared on Earth. Plants cannot move from place to place like animals. Wind and water helped to spread them around the world. Many plants were spread by animals.

Today, there are plants living almost everywhere on the Earth, from the humid rain forests and hot deserts to the windy mountaintops and freezing polar regions.

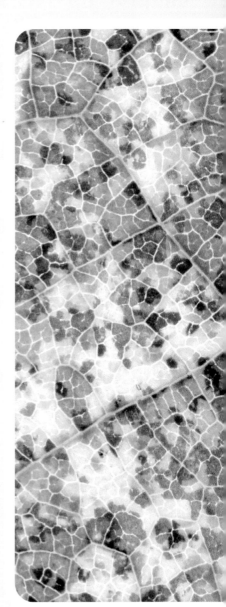

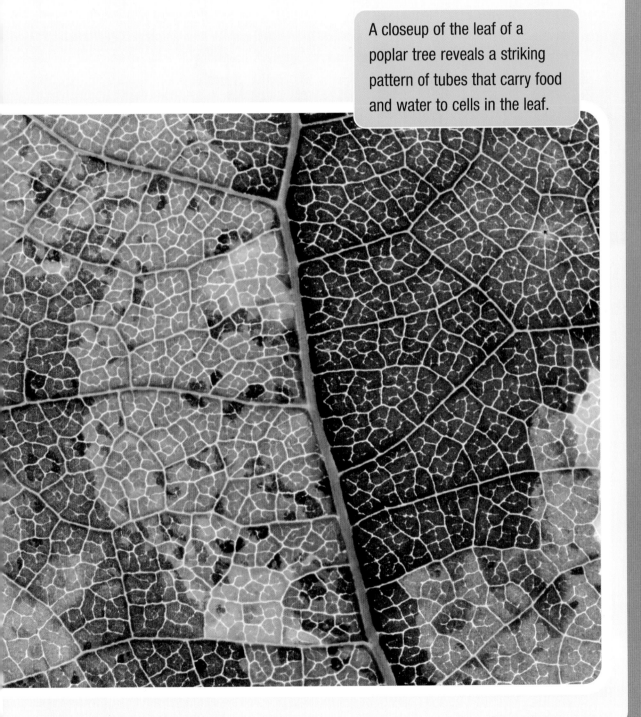

A closeup of the leaf of a poplar tree reveals a striking pattern of tubes that carry food and water to cells in the leaf.

CHAPTER 1

Little Boxes

Almost all living things are made up of one or more little boxes called cells. Cells are the smallest units of life. Some plants are made up of just one cell. Others, such as an oak tree, contain billions of cells. In plants, one cell can divide into two new cells so that plants can grow and repair themselves.

Plant cells share many features with animal cells. Both types of cells are enclosed in a fatty layer called a **cell membrane**. There is a **nucleus** inside both plant and animal cells. The nucleus is the cell's "brain." It controls the processes that go on inside the cell.

Plant cells and animal cells are not exactly the same. Unlike animal cells, plant cells have rigid cell walls. This protects the plant and helps it to keep its shape. Unlike animal cells, many plant cells have tiny sacs called **chloroplasts**. These sacs help plants make their food.

Plant cells come in many shapes and sizes depending on what they do. Cells that do similar jobs join up to form tissues. Examples of plant tissues are the tubes for carrying food and water inside the plant. Tissues that do similar jobs join up to form organs. Examples of plant organs are leaves or flowers.

The rigid walls of these plant cells make up the stem and help the plant to hold itself upright. These cells are from a stinging nettle.

Inside a Plant Cell

There is a lot going on inside a plant cell. Chemical reactions take place, and the cell makes food. The energy produced by these reactions keeps the cell working properly.

Cell contents

The plant cell wall is tough and rigid. It is made up of layers of a rubbery substance called **cellulose**. Underneath the cell wall is a cell membrane. This thin layer of fat seals off the cell from the outside world. The cell membrane controls what goes in and out of the cell. Inside this membrane, the cell is full of a liquid called **cytoplasm**. Thin threads of cytoplasm pass through the cell wall and link one cell with the next. Several tiny objects, called **organelles**, can be found floating in the cytoplasm. One of the most obvious is called a vacuole. This storage sac holds the cell's waste products before they are removed from the cell.

This cell has been taken from the root of a maize plant. The thin cell wall (pale green) is clearly visible. The large red object inside the cell is the nucleus.

Jobs in the cell

The control center of a cell is the nucleus. The nucleus directs the

Close Up

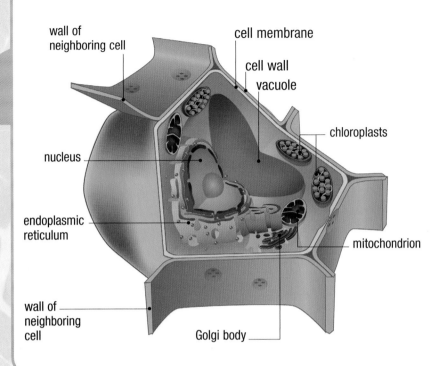

wall of neighboring cell

cell membrane

cell wall

vacuole

chloroplasts

nucleus

endoplasmic reticulum

mitochondrion

wall of neighboring cell

Golgi body

Every plant cell is surrounded by a tough layer called a cell wall. Under that is the cell membrane, which encloses the cell's contents. Inside the cell are organelles such as chloroplasts, the nucleus, a Golgi body, mitochondria, and a vacuole.

processes that go on inside the cell. Different organelles have different tasks to do. Organelles known as chloroplasts trap energy from the Sun to make food. **Mitochondria** (*singular* mitochondrion) release energy from the food. A membrane called the endoplasmic reticulum makes and stores substances such as **proteins**, which help the cell to function. The Golgi body collects these proteins and transports them through the cell membrane.

Fast Facts

● The vacuole in a plant cell takes in water and presses against the cell wall. This helps the cell to keep its shape. A vacuole may fill up most of the space of a cell.

● Lying one on top of the other, 10,000 cell membranes would be the same thickness as this page.

How Plants Grow

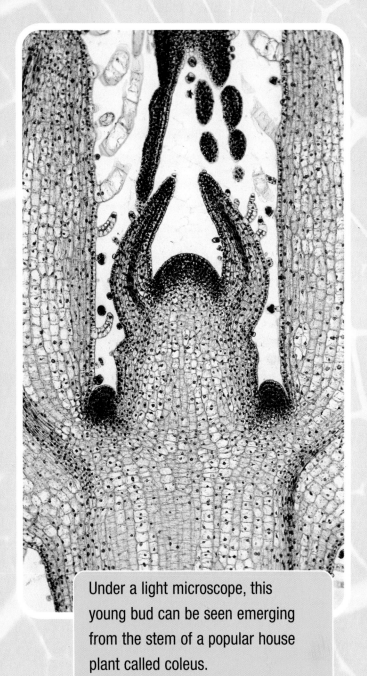

Under a light microscope, this young bud can be seen emerging from the stem of a popular house plant called coleus.

Plants grow through a process called **cell division**. One cell divides into two new cells. The new cells then grow to the size of the original cell. This makes the plant bigger. Plants can also grow when existing cells increase in size.

Stop and grow

Some plant parts, such as the leaves, can only grow to a certain size. Others, such as the roots and stems, grow for the plant's whole life. The roots and stems contain cell clusters called **meristems**. The meristems keep dividing to produce new cells.

Apical meristems lie at the tips of the plant's roots and shoots. These cells make the plant grow longer. A plant that lives for one or two years grows mainly in height. Plants that live for many years, such as trees, grow thicker as well as longer. These plants have extra meristems, called lateral meristems. These cells form extra tubes to carry water and food toward the middle of the plant. They

Tiny Trees

Bonsai is the name given to the ancient art of growing tiny trees. People grow bonsai trees in small pots. Over many years, the roots and branches of the bonsai trees are carefully trimmed. The aim is to grow a tree that ranges from 2 inches (5 centimeters) to about 2 feet (60 cm) tall. Similar to normal trees, bonsai trees may live for 100 years or more.

also form more protective tissue, such as bark, around the outside.

alive from year to year, growing longer and thicker.

Life spans

Some plants live longer than others. Plants that live for one growing season are called annuals. Plants that live for two seasons are called biennials (*bi* means "two"). Others, called perennials, live for several seasons. Some perennials die back to the base every year and grow fresh shoots the following year. Others have woody stems that stay

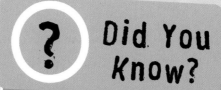

? Did You Know?

The world's fastest-growing plant is a giant bamboo, which may grow up to 3 feet (90 centimeters) in one day. Some bamboo plants have even been heard to make squeaking and creaking noises as they grow.

CHAPTER 2

Plant Parts

There are three main parts to most plants: the stem, the roots, and the leaves. Many plants also have parts to help them reproduce, or make new plants. These include cones and flowers, which are made up of special leaves.

The roots hold the plant in place in the soil. Roots are not usually visible because they grow under the ground. The most important job of the roots is to absorb water and minerals from the soil. A system of tiny tubes inside the root carries these nutrients to the stem. Some plants, such as carrots and potatoes, also store food in their roots.

The stem is usually a long, thin tube that links the roots to the leaves. The stem usually grows upward and supports the plant's weight. Like the roots, the stem acts like a transport system. It carries water and food between the roots and the leaves. It does this through a series of tubes that line the stem.

The leaves are important because they make food for the plant. The leaves have transport tubes inside, so the food made there can travel to all other parts of the plant. These tubes show up as a striking pattern of lines and ridges on the surface of the leaf.

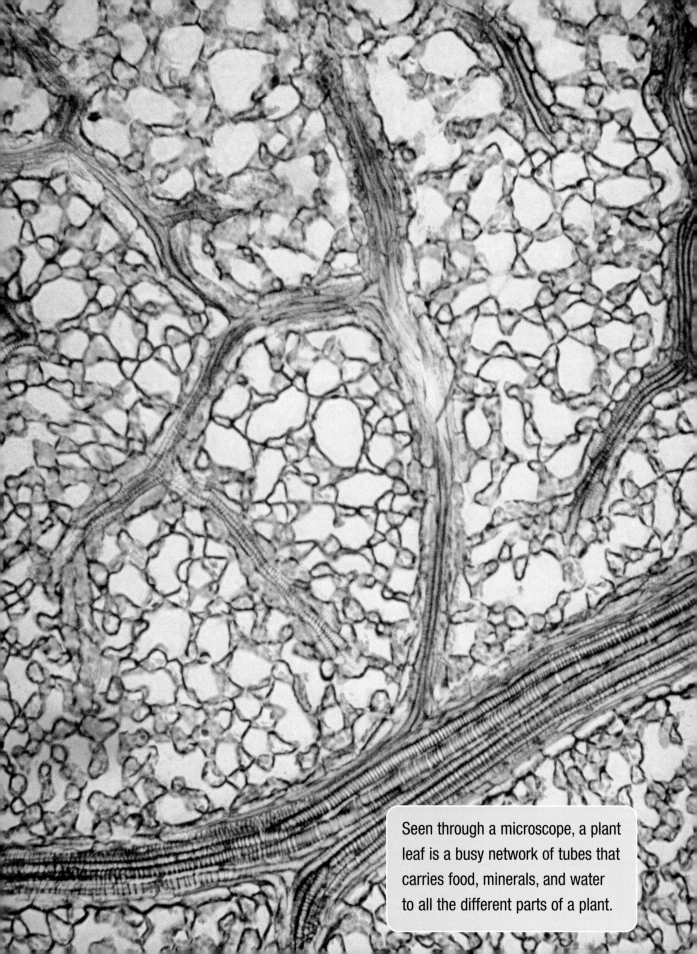

Seen through a microscope, a plant leaf is a busy network of tubes that carries food, minerals, and water to all the different parts of a plant.

Rooting Around.

The food tubes (pink) and water tubes (orange) form a strong, but flexible, core in a root so the root can bend as it pushes its way through the soil.

A plant's roots are a network of thin threadlike tissues that absorb water and minerals from the soil. Root hairs may cover the roots. These increase the surface area through which to absorb these substances.

A root grows when the cells near the tip of the root divide into two new cells. This area of new cell growth is known as the "zone of elongation." As the new cells grow, they stretch and push the root through the soil.

- The deepest roots in the plant world belong to a wild fig tree in South Africa. The roots grow to a depth of 395 feet (120 meters).

- The longest roots belong to a plant called rye grass. The roots can stretch up to 387 miles (623 kilometers) through the soil.

Root type

Roots come in many shapes and sizes. A tap root is large and grows straight down, with many side shoots called lateral roots. Fibrous roots are a mass of roots of different sizes. Lateral roots are all a similar size.

Some roots are unusual because they grow above ground. Buttress roots look like planks of wood growing out from the bottom of trees. They support trees that grow in loose, thin soil, such as in the rain forest. Prop roots help to support plants such as mangroves, which often grow partly underwater in slippery mud. Prop roots grow out from a stem and then arch down into the ground. Ivy plants use their prop roots for climbing.

Some roots do not grow in the ground at all. Some orchids perch high on the trees of the rain forest. Their roots hang down from the branches and soak up water from the air. They are called aerial roots (*aerial* means "in the air").

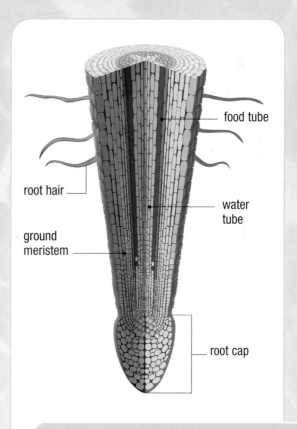

food tube

root hair

water tube

ground meristem

root cap

Tough cells make up the pointed root cap. These cells protect the root tip and help it push through the soil.

Stem Support

The stem does many jobs for a plant. It holds the leaves, flowers, or cones above the ground. It houses tubes through which food and water travel to different parts of the plant. The stem also stores food and water. It makes new cells as the plant grows.

Big plants, such as trees, have thick, woody stems for extra support. The main stem of a tree is the trunk. A short woody plant with many stems close to the ground is called a shrub. Smaller plants with green stems use the pressure of the watery sap inside their cells to stay upright. This is why plants droop, or wilt, if you forget to water them.

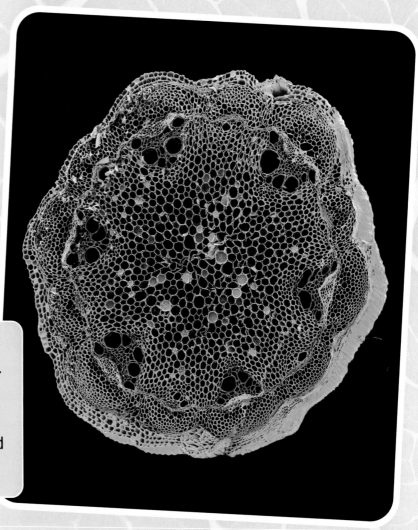

This image shows cells in the stem of a clematis. There are bundles of food tubes (yellow) and water tubes (blue) around the edge of the stem.

Patterns inside plants

In the stems of some young plants, the food and water tubes cluster at the edges of the stem. As the plant grows older, the clusters join up to form a ring. This makes the stem strong but springy, so that it can bend in the wind without breaking. In other plants, the clusters of tubes are spread throughout the stem in no regular pattern.

Underground stems

Some plants store food in swollen underground stems. When the growing season is over, the plant dies back to the base. The plant grows back the next season, using

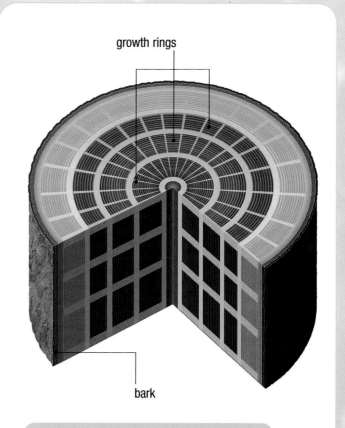

growth rings

bark

A growth ring on a tree trunk shows how much the tree grew in one year. The bark keeps out diseases and stops the tree from drying out.

? Did You Know?

The stems of stinging nettles are covered in sharp hairs, which are full of poison. Each hair is just one long, thin cell. The hair acts like a tiny needle to inject an irritating chemical into an animal's skin.

the food stored in the stem. Bulbs are underground stems wrapped in leaves and swollen with stored food. Potatoes are the swollen tips of underground stems. They are called tubers. The "eyes" on a potato tuber are tiny buds that sprout stems and grow into new potato plants.

Catching the Light

Leaves take in energy from sunlight and use it to make food for the plant. A plant will arrange the leaves in a pattern to catch as much sunlight as possible without casting shadows over the other leaves. A typical leaf is made up of a thin, flat blade called a lamina. The lamina provides a large area for catching the light. The lamina is joined to the stem by a stalk called a petiole. A leaf divided into two or more smaller leaves is called a compound leaf.

Cell Invaders

Plant cells are often invaded by tiny particles called viruses. Viruses cannot pass through the tough plant cell wall by themselves. Instead, they hitch a ride with fungi, insects, and worms that enter or break apart the plant. Some viruses kill plants. Others damage parts such as the leaves.

Vein patterns

The leaf blade is strengthened by veins, which are bundles of water and food tubes. The main vein is called the midrib. In most plants, the veins form a web throughout the leaf. In others, such as grasses, the veins run parallel to the midrib.

Leaf layers

A leaf consists of layers of different types of cells. On the outside is the **epidermis**, which is just one cell thick. The epidermis is covered by a see-through, waterproof layer, called a **cuticle**. The cuticle stops the leaf from losing too much water. On the inside of the leaf is a thick layer of mesophyll cells. Near the leaf's surface are the tightly packed palisade mesophyll cells. These cells are shaped like columns and make food for the plant. Underneath are the spongy mesophyll cells, which are loosely packed and have air spaces between them. Running through the layer of mesophyll cells are the food and water tubes. These tubes run down the leaf stalk and into the stem.

Unusual leaves

Leaves come in many shapes and sizes. One desert plant has leaves that look like tiny pebbles! This adaptation helps to hide it from hungry animals that cannot see these plants among the real pebbles on the desert floor. This plant is called the living stone.

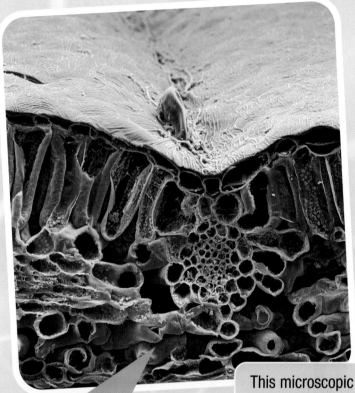

This microscopic cross-section of a leaf shows the layers of different cells. The mesophyll cells make up most of the leaf.

Close Up

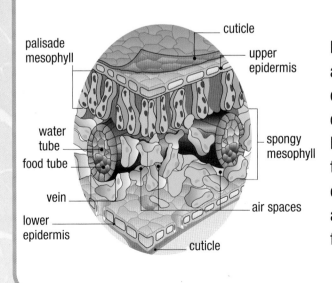

palisade mesophyll
cuticle
upper epidermis
water tube
food tube
spongy mesophyll
vein
air spaces
lower epidermis
cuticle

Inside a leaf are layers of different types of cells. The cell layers work together to collect sunlight and make food for the plant.

CHAPTER 3

Making Food

Animals cannot make their own food like plants can. Most animals depend on plants or other animals for food. Some eat only plants, while others eat plant-eating animals. Without plants, nothing could survive on Earth.

Plants make food in organelles called chloroplasts inside their leaves. The chloroplasts trap the energy from sunlight and use it to produce sugars from two simple ingredients. The first is a gas called carbon dioxide, which is found in small amounts in the air. The second ingredient is water. This process of making food is called **photosynthesis**, which means "making things with light."

The sugary food that plants make through photosynthesis is called sap. Food tubes form a network in the leaves and carry the sap to the main stem. From there, it can be shipped around the plant to the cells that need it most. The thick, liquid sap is packed with energy. Some of the energy is used right away to keep the plant healthy and ensure it is working properly. Some of the energy is stored away for later use. And some of it is changed into other substances that the plant needs, such as proteins.

The chloroplasts (shown here as green structures) inside plant cells trap the energy from the Sun. The energy is used to combine carbon dioxide and water into sugary food.

Sugar Factories

The chloroplasts inside plant cells are like miniature factories. The raw materials needed for these tiny factories are water and a gas in the air called carbon dioxide. Each chloroplast uses the energy from sunlight to combine carbon dioxide with water to make substances called **carbohydrates**. These carbohydrates are types of sugar and store energy for the plant. Plants take in carbon dioxide through tiny holes in their leaves.

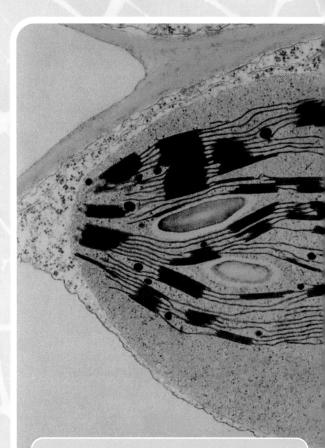

The chloroplasts inside plant cells are the site of photosynthesis. One plant cell may contain between one and one hundred chloroplasts.

Fast Facts

- The word *chloroplast* comes from the Greek words *chloros*, meaning "green," and *plastos*, which means "formed."

- Leaves look greenish-yellow because chlorophyll absorbs the blue, red, and violet parts of white light and reflects the green.

The water they need to make the food usually comes from the soil. The plant's roots absorb water from the soil, and the water travels up the

Close Up

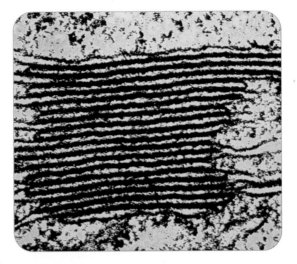

The membranes inside a chloroplast form hollow, disc-shaped sacs called thylakoids. The thylakoids stack on top of each other like piles of coins (left). A stack of thylakoids is called a granum (*plural* grana).

plants need oxygen to release the stored energy from the carbohydrate food.

Inside a chloroplast

A chloroplast is an oval sac. It is surrounded and protected by an envelope of two membranes. These membranes control the movement of substances into and out of the chloroplast. Inside the chloroplast is a grainy fluid called the stroma (where sugars are made) and sheetlike membranes packed with **chlorophyll** (a green substance that traps energy from sunlight).

stem and through the veins in the leaves. Plants that live in water take in water and carbon dioxide gas all over their surface.

When plants make carbohydrates, oxygen is given off as waste. This is useful because both animals and

Food on the Move

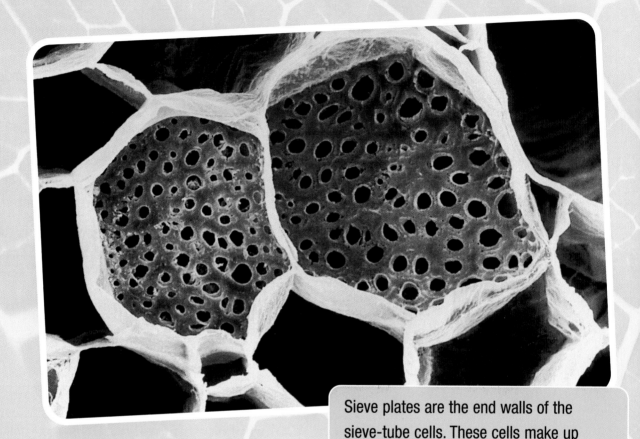

Sieve plates are the end walls of the sieve-tube cells. These cells make up phloem tissue in plants with flowers.

Have you ever seen sap dripping from a wound in a tree trunk? This sap is the plant's sugary food, and it comes from food tubes called **phloem**. The phloem carries food from the leaves to all parts of the plant. The food may be needed to help the plant grow, or it may be sent to storage structures, such as bulbs or tubers, for later use.

Phloem is always bundled together with the tubes that carry water around the plant.

Phloem parts

Phloem is usually made of different types of cells, including sieve-tube cells, companion cells, and phloem fibers. In plants with flowers, sieve-tube cells join up to form columns of cells called sieve tubes. The word *sieve* refers to the holes in the end walls of the sieve-tube cells. These end walls look like a kitchen sieve or strainer and are called sieve plates. They help to move the food through phloem. The cells that make up the sieve tube do not have nuclei. They are controlled and kept alive by neighboring companion cells, which do have nuclei. The companion cells are connected to the sieve-tube cells by tiny threads of cytoplasm.

In plants that do not have flowers, the phloem is made up of sieve-tube cells with holes in all their walls, not just at the ends of the cells.

? Did You Know?

Aphids (also called greenflies) jab their sharp mouthparts into a plant's phloem tubes to suck up the sugary sap. The sugars the aphids do not need are pushed out of their bodies as drops of sticky honeydew.

Tree phloem

In trees, the phloem makes up the inside layer of bark. Animals often tear bark to reach the sap in the phloem. If they strip off a ring of bark around the trunk, food cannot reach the roots, and the tree dies.

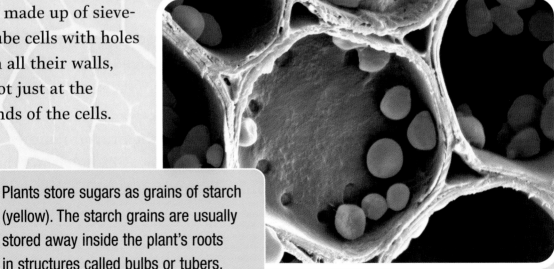

Plants store sugars as grains of starch (yellow). The starch grains are usually stored away inside the plant's roots in structures called bulbs or tubers.

CHAPTER 4

Air and Water

Plants need air and water to stay alive. They need gases in the air to make and release the energy from their food. Plants also need water for all the chemical reactions that occur inside their cells and to help the cells keep their shape. Water also helps plants keep a steady temperature.

Air passes through most plants through tiny holes, called **stomata** (*singular* stoma), in the leaves. Plants with juicy, green stems have these stomata in their stems as well as in the leaves. Some plants with woody stems also have raised pores, called lenticels, in the stem. When water travels up the plant's water tubes, from the roots to the leaves, it often leaks through the stomata. This is similar to a person sweating through his or her skin. Plants control the flow of air and water through a leaf or green stem by opening or closing their stomata.

Two bean-shaped cells, called guard cells, help the stomata open or close. When the guard cells absorb water, the pressure of the water makes the cells bulge and the stomata open up to let air into the plant. The guard cells shrink when they lose water, which draws the stomata tightly shut.

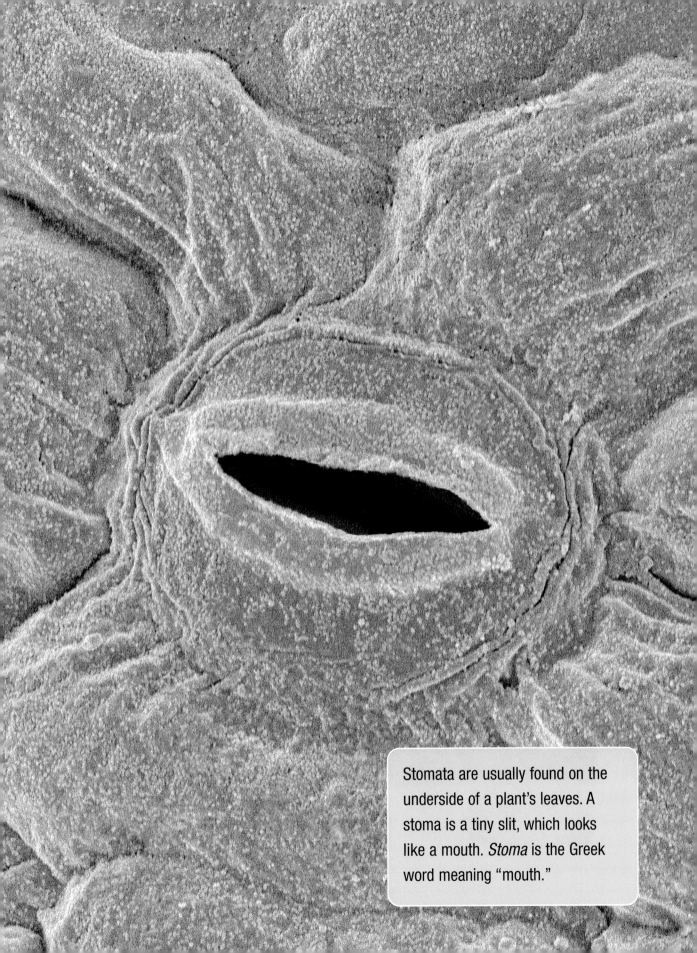

Stomata are usually found on the underside of a plant's leaves. A stoma is a tiny slit, which looks like a mouth. *Stoma* is the Greek word meaning "mouth."

Water Tubes

The tubes that carry water and minerals from a plant's roots to its leaves are called **xylem**. Xylem is made of long, hollow cells with thick walls. The walls of the cells have holes to allow water to move from cell to cell. The cells are joined end to end to form tubes that go all the way up the plant. Fully grown xylem cells are dead, unlike the phloem cells, which are living.

Moving water

Water always moves up through a plant. There is a pulling force from above and a smaller pushing force from below. The pulling force occurs as water escapes through stomata in the leaves and stem. Water tends to stick together, so as it moves out of the stomata, more water is pulled up to take its place. This process is called **transpiration**.

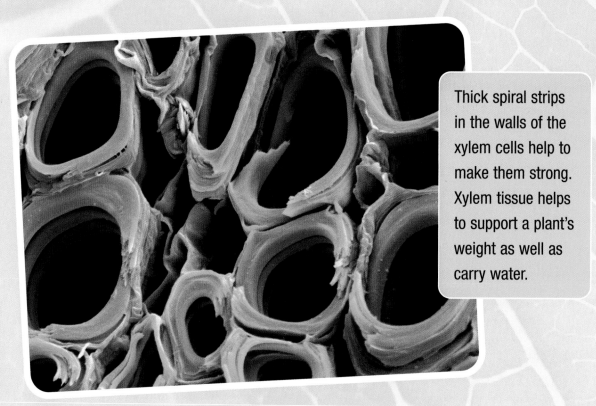

Thick spiral strips in the walls of the xylem cells help to make them strong. Xylem tissue helps to support a plant's weight as well as carry water.

Close Up

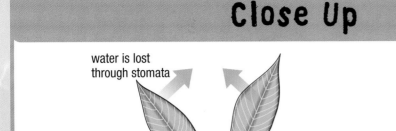

water is lost through stomata

a pulling force sucks water up into the leaves

root pressure pushes water partly up the stem

water is absorbed through the roots

The upward flow of water through the xylem is called the transpiration stream. The water moves up to replace the water lost through the tiny stomata in the stem and leaves.

The pushing force comes from the roots of the plant. As the roots absorb water, pressure builds and pushes the water into the stem. Root pressure can only push water a little way up the stem, and it does not happen in all plants. The pulling force takes care of the rest.

Winter water

In areas with cold winters, the water in the ground may freeze. Some trees with wide, flat leaves cannot get enough water. These trees drop their leaves in winter. Without their leaves, the trees need less water.

So the trees shut down for the winter and grow new leaves in spring, when the frozen ground thaws. Then they can drink up water from the soil again.

Fast Facts

- On a warm day, a large tree may absorb 250 gallons (950 liters) of water from the soil.

- The xylem in some vines and trees may be many yards long.

Adapting to Water

Many plants live submerged in the water or in very wet places, such as the tropical rain forest where it rains nearly every day. Other plants live in very dry places, where it hardly ever rains. In some deserts, there may be no rainstorms for several years.

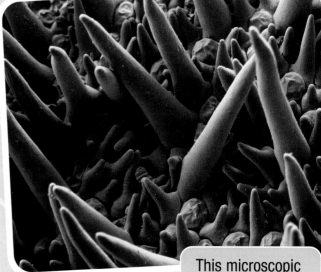

This microscopic picture shows the sharp spines on the surface of a cactus plant. The tiny stomata are hidden under the small bumps on the stem of the cactus.

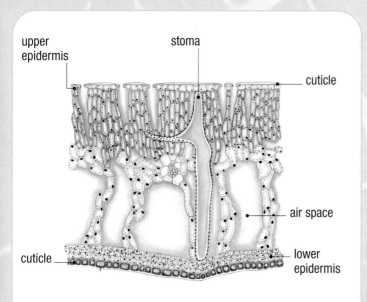

upper epidermis

stoma

cuticle

cuticle

air space

lower epidermis

This view inside a water lily leaf shows the air spaces that help the leaf float. The stomata are on the upper surface of the leaf to take in air from above the water.

Water plants

Water lilies are well suited to a life in a lake or pond. These plants do not need strong stems, since the water supports the weight of the plant. Water runs off the tough, waxy leaves to stop the plants from having too much water. The long, bendy leaf stalks allow the leaves to adapt to changes in water level. They float on the water's surface to catch the sunlight, while the roots anchor the water lilies in the mud.

Some water plants float freely on the water's surface. Tiny roots hang from the leaves of these plants and take in minerals from the water. Many plants that live in rain forests have leaves with pointed tips so that water easily drips off.

Desert plants

The dry, scorching desert is a harsh place for plants to live. Some, such as mesquite trees, have long roots so they can tap into the water stored deep underground. Others, such as cacti, store water in swollen stems and have spreading roots to absorb as much water from the dry soil as possible. Cacti have spines instead

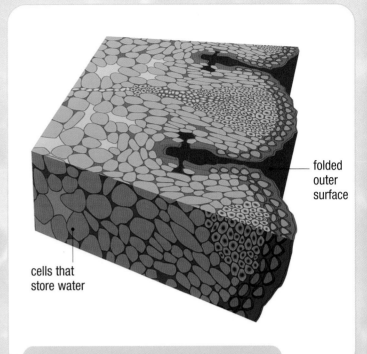

folded outer surface

cells that store water

A slice through a saguaro cactus shows the folded surface of the stem. The stem is full of cells that store water. The stem expands when it rains.

of leaves, and their stomata are sunk in deep pits so that less water escapes into the air. Flowering uses up a lot of water, so desert cacti usually only flower in the short rainy season.

Another desert survival trick includes lying in the sand as seeds until it rains, then quickly growing, flowering, and making seeds before the ground dries out again.

Fast Facts

● The leaves of the giant water lily from the Amazon can grow up to 7.5 feet (2.3 m) across.

● Up to 90 percent of the weight of a cactus is water.

CHAPTER 5

Seeds and Spores

A plant begins life as a seed or a spore. These tiny packages of plant life may be carried away from the parent plant by the wind, water currents, or animals that eat the plants and deposit the seeds elsewhere in their feces. This spreading is called seed dispersal, and it gives a young plant a better chance of survival. The seed or spore will sprout into a new plant if it lands in a warm, moist place.

Seeds are produced by plants with flowers and plants with cones. A seed is made up of a baby plant, called an embryo, and a food store. The seed is surrounded by a tough coat called a testa. The testa helps to protect the embryo from diseases and pests. The seeds produced by plants with flowers are enclosed inside a protective case called a **fruit**. Many fruits, such as grapes, are fleshy and juicy. Other fruits, such as pecans, are hard and dry. Plants with cones do not form fruits. Their seeds are protected by the scales of the cones.

Spores are produced by plants such as ferns and mosses. A spore is smaller and much simpler than a seed. The spore usually consists of one cell surrounded by a tough coat, and it has no embryo or food store.

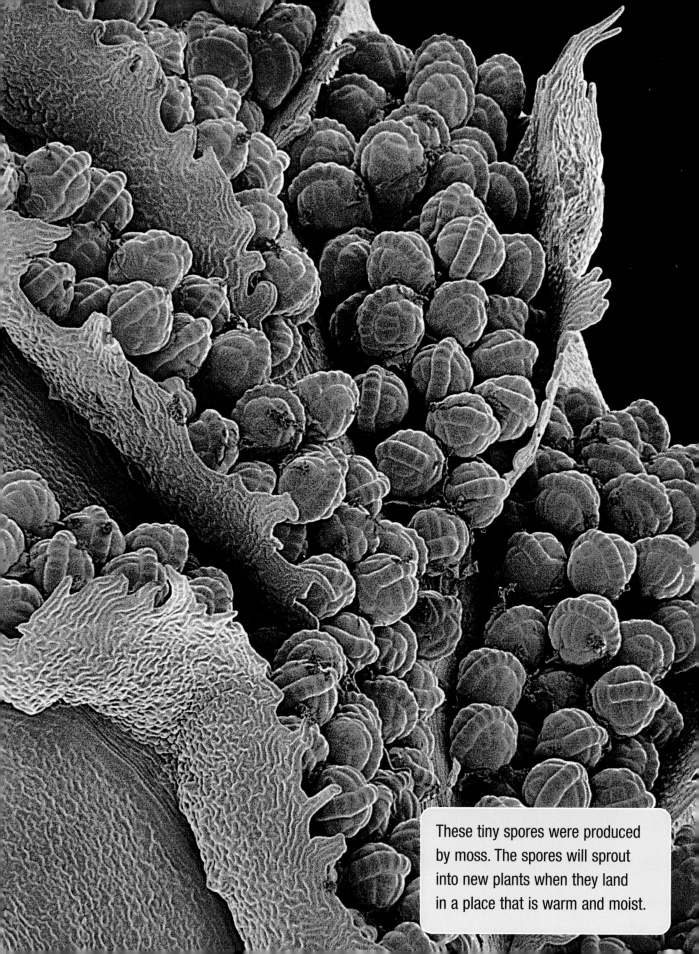

These tiny spores were produced by moss. The spores will sprout into new plants when they land in a place that is warm and moist.

Spreading Seeds and Spores

Seeds and spores are often small, light, and easy to move to a new home. It is good for a new plant to grow away from home. Otherwise the new plant would have to compete with the parent plant for space, light, and nutrients.

Do-it-yourself dispersal

Some plants spread their own seeds. The fruits burst open, flinging seeds in all directions. When jewel weed fruits are ripe they suddenly burst open, sending the seeds flying several feet away.

↑ This cocklebur fruit is stuck in a raccoon's fur. The fruit will fall off and may grow into a new plant.

A dandelion seed can → be blown as far as 6 miles (10 km) in the wind.

Fast Facts

- Orchid seeds are so small that they drift like dust in the air.

- A large fern may produce several hundred million spores a year.

Wind and water

The spores of ferns and mosses are light. They can float in the wind. Many plants with cones and some plants with flowers also use the wind to spread their seeds. The seeds may have sails, wings, or tiny parachute-like structures to glide through the air. The seeds of maple and sycamore trees spin like helicopters as they are blown in the wind.

The seeds of plants that grow in or by the water may use water to spread to new places. Their seeds and fruits have waterproof coats and

A fern plant produces spores in a case called a sporangium. When the spores are ripe, the sporangium breaks open. The spores then shoot out into the air.

float to stay on the surface. Coconut palms grow by the ocean. Their fruits (coconuts) may be carried by the water to new shores.

Hitching a ride

Some plant seeds hitch a ride on animals. The cocklebur fruit hooks to the animal's fur. The fruit can be carried many miles before it falls off. Animals also eat many fruits. As the fruit passes through the animal, the testa protect the seeds. The seeds are then excreted from the animal's body in feces. The seeds grow into new plants, using the feces for nutrients.

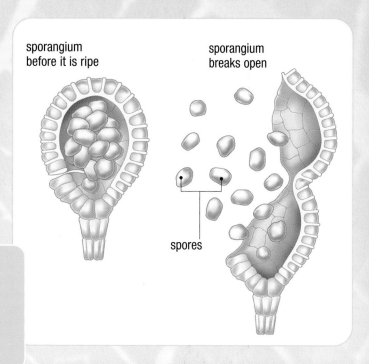

sporangium before it is ripe

sporangium breaks open

spores

Sprouting Seeds and Spores

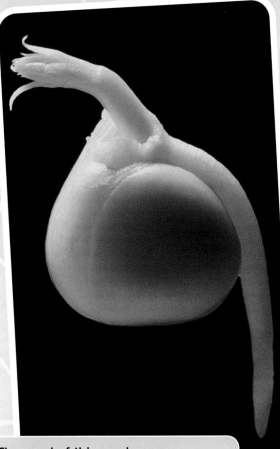

The seeds of some plants may rest, or stay dormant, for days, months, or even years before they start to grow into new plants. When the conditions are right, the seeds then sprout roots and leaves, using the energy from the food stored in the seed. This process is called **germination**, and it begins when the seed takes in water and swells up. The testa then splits open. A young root, called a **radicle**, emerges and grows down into the soil. Soon a **shoot**, or plumule, begins to grow up toward the light.

The seed of this garden pea has germinated. The shoot has emerged and is growing up toward the light. The radicle is growing downward. The two cotyledons are the two halves of the body of the pea, and they remain underground.

The first leaves

The first leaves of a plant with flowers are called seed leaves or **cotyledons**. The cotyledons are held inside the seeds until germination, when they may rise above the ground. The cotyledons' shape is often different from the shape of the normal leaves that grow later.

Many plants with flowers have two cotyledons (such as sunflowers), but some have only one (such as grasses).

In some plants with flowers, such as peas and beans, the cotyledons stay underground. This is called hypogeal germination. In other plants with flowers, such as sunflowers, the cotyledons push up above the ground. The cotyledons become the first green leaves, and they start to make food for the plant through photosynthesis. This is known as epigeal germination.

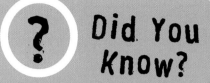

? Did You Know?

Seeds of a water plant called Indian, or sacred, lotus germinated after lying in a dried lake bed in China for more than 1,200 years.

Spore germination

The spores from plants such as ferns do not grow into new plants right away. First, they grow into thin, often heart-shaped leaflike mats, called prothalli, on the ground. These produce female eggs and male sperm, which join to form an embryo of a new fern plant.

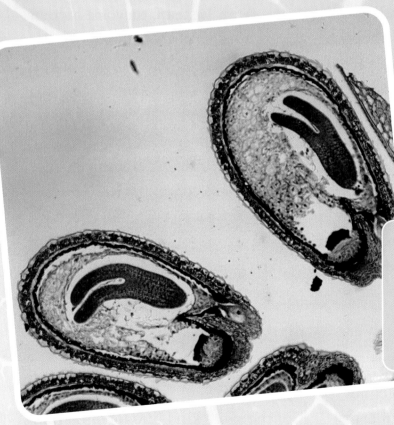

This image shows the seeds of a shepherd's purse. The seeds may rest in the soil for 35 years or more before they start to grow.

CHAPTER 6

Cones and Flowers

Cones and flowers produce seeds for plants. Before a seed can develop, a male cell must join with a female cell. These cells may be from the same plant or from another plant of the same kind.

Male cells are found inside tiny grains called **pollen**. Only the male parts of plants with cones or flowers make the pollen grains. The female cells, called eggs, are found inside a structure called an ovule. In plants with flowers, the ovules are protected inside a chamber called an ovary. The ovary wall develops into a fruit. In plants with cones, the ovules are not inside an ovary

or a fruit. Instead, they are hidden in the scales of the cones.

Water currents, animals such as insects, and strong winds carry the pollen to the female parts of flowers or cones. This pollen transfer is called **pollination**. If animals do it they are called pollinators. Flowers often make a sugary food called nectar to "reward" their pollinators. Many plants have male and female parts in one flower and can pollinate themselves (self pollination). Plants try to avoid this. Stronger plants are produced if pollen from one plant joins with ovules on another plant of the same kind (cross pollination).

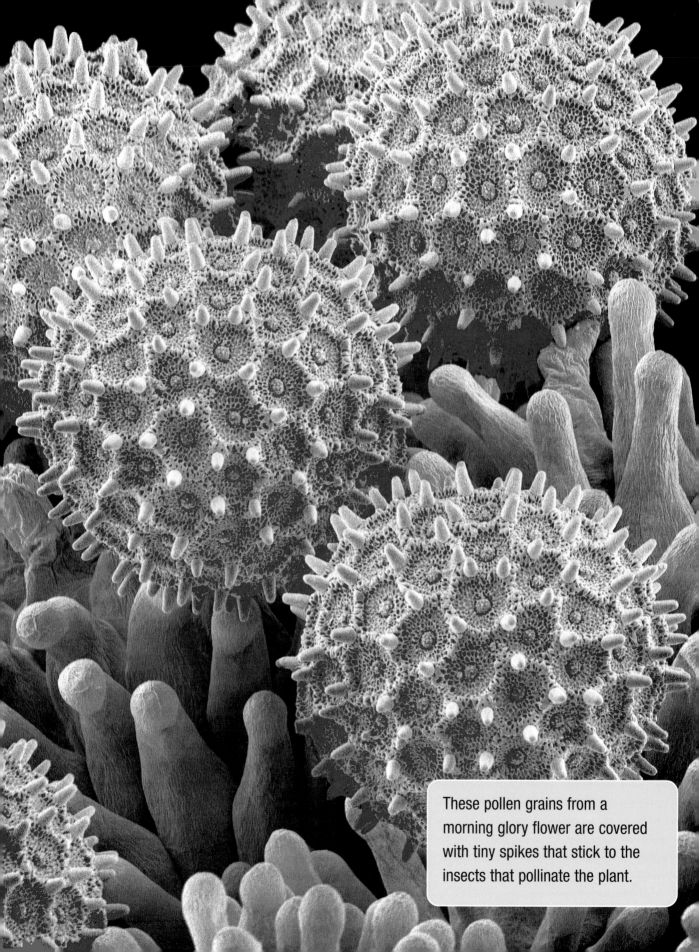

These pollen grains from a morning glory flower are covered with tiny spikes that stick to the insects that pollinate the plant.

Plants with Cones

Plants with cones were the first plants to reproduce using seeds. Their cones are made from special leaves called scales. The cones are either male or female, and they usually grow on the same plant. They are named for their often conelike shape.

A pine tree releases a cloud of pollen. The pollen grains land on another tree where they pollinate it.

Male cones

Male cones are produced each year. They make pollen in special sacs, called microsporangia, attached to their scales. The wind then blows the pollen away. Wind pollination happens by chance, so a lot of pollen is made to ensure some of it reaches the female cones.

Female cones

A female cone is small and soft at first. It takes between six months and two years to grow into a hard,

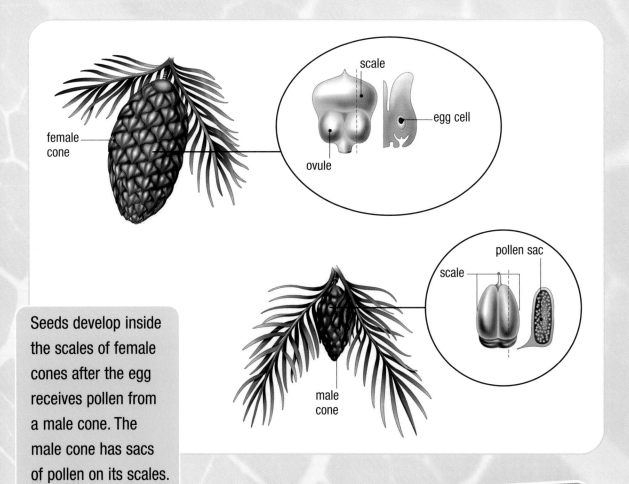

female cone

scale

egg cell

ovule

pollen sac

scale

male cone

Seeds develop inside the scales of female cones after the egg receives pollen from a male cone. The male cone has sacs of pollen on its scales.

ripe cone full of seeds. Ovules in the scales of the female cone receive pollen. Male cells then join with female cells in the ovules. The scales harden and close, and seeds develop. When the seeds are fully grown, the scales separate or fall off and release the seeds. The seeds then drift away on the wind or are eaten by animals.

Fast Facts

● The wind can blow pollen more than 3,000 miles (4,800 km).

● Pollen blowing through the air gives some people itchy, watery eyes and makes them sneeze. This reaction to pollen is known as hay fever.

Flowering Plants

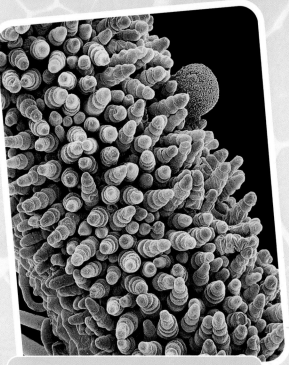

Like cones, flowers are made from special leaves. Unlike cones, there are usually male and female parts in the same flower.

Flower structure

A typical flower consists of four rings. The outer ring, or calyx, is

This microscopic picture shows a stigma from a geranium flower. It is covered in sticky bumps to trap pollen.

The female parts of this apple flower are called carpels and include the stigmas, styles, and ovaries. The male parts of the flower are called stamens. They are made up of anthers and filaments.

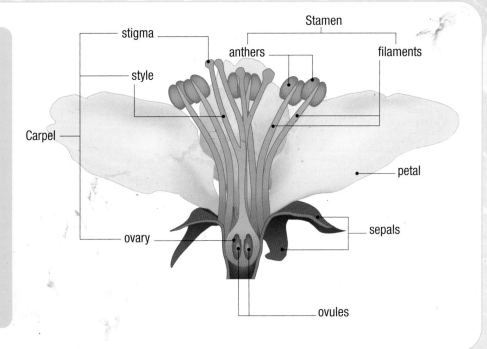

stigma

Stamen

anthers

filaments

style

Carpel

petal

ovary

sepals

ovules

Water Pollination

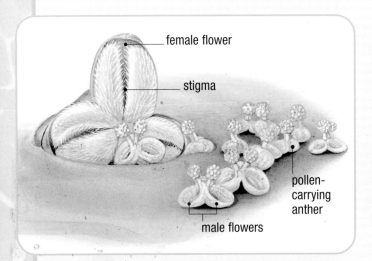

female flower

stigma

pollen-carrying anther

male flowers

In the summer, water celery grows long flower stalks with female flowers that rest on the surface of the water. Male flowers are produced underwater and then rise and rest on the water's surface. The wind and water currents then push the male flowers toward the female flowers so that pollination can happen.

made of protective flaps called sepals. Next comes the flower's corolla, which is a ring of petals. Inside the corolla is a ring of male parts. Inside this is an inner ring of female parts.

Inner ring

The male parts of a flower are called stamens. Each stamen consists of a stalk called a filament with a sac of pollen, called an anther, on the end. The female parts of a flower are called carpels. Each carpel is made up of a sticky tip called a stigma (that catches pollen) on top of a

stalk called a style. Below the style is the flower's ovary, which contains the ovules. The ovules develop into seeds if they receive pollen from a flower of the same species.

Fast Facts

● The world's biggest flower is around 3 feet (1 m) across and belongs to the *Rafflesia* plant.

● A sunflower contains up to 2,000 smaller flowers, called florets.

Flowers to Fruits

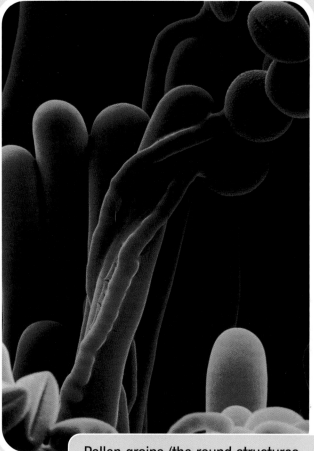

When a pollen grain from one plant lands on a female cone or the stigma of another flowering plant, it grows a very fine tube called a pollen tube. The pollen tube grows down to meet the ovule. The pollen grain then joins with the female cell, or egg, inside the ovule. This process is called fertilization, and it means that a seed can start to develop.

In plants with flowers, two male pollen grains travel down the pollen tube to meet the ovules. One male cell fertilizes the egg, while the other male cell joins with another egg to produce endosperm. Endosperm is a food store for the developing seed. When two male cells fertilize two eggs, it is called double fertilization. This can only happen in plants with flowers.

Pollen grains (the round structures at the top of the picture) land on the stigma (the long, tubelike structures) of a poppy flower. Fertilization takes place when the male cell fuses with the female egg inside the ovule.

From flower to seed

After fertilization, flowers no longer need most of their parts. The petals, stamens, stigma, and style shrivel up and usually drop off the flower.

- Some plants in the pea family produce seed pods that are more than 5 feet (1.5 m) long.

- The world's biggest fruit comes from a palm called Coco-de-mer and weighs up to 44 pounds (20 kilograms).

The sepals may stay to protect the ovary. The seeds develop inside the ovary, which develops into a fruit.

Fantastic fruits

A simple fruit forms from one ovary and may have one large seed (for example, a peach) or many small seeds (for example, a tomato). Compound fruits develop from several joined ovaries. Each segment of an orange forms from one ovary. False fruits, such as apples, are made from an ovary as well as other flower parts. The part of an apple that people eat is the **receptacle**. The receptacle swells up around the ovary, which is the core of the apple. The core is the true fruit.

Conclusion

Plants come in many different shapes and sizes. They live in different parts of the world, and they reproduce in different ways. But all plants share one important feature. They are made up of tiny building blocks called cells.

Cells are so small that scientists need to use microscopes to look at them. Simple microscopes reveal tiny organelles, such as the nucleus, hidden inside the cell. Powerful electron microscopes reveal even smaller structures inside these organelles, such as the tiny strands of DNA inside the nucleus.

The invisible world of the cell is the driving force behind all plants. Chemical reactions that take place inside cells control plant processes. These include making food for the plant by using energy from the Sun, and helping new cells to grow. These reactions also produce the amazing variety of colorful leaves, fragrant flowers, and tasty vegetables and fruits that people grow and eat.

Glossary

carbohydrates These sugars are made up of the elements carbon, hydrogen, and oxygen.

cell division A biological process called cell division is when one cell divides into two new cells.

cell membrane A thin cell membrane inside the cell wall seals off the cell from the outside.

cellulose A chemical called cellulose is made up of chains of sugars.

chlorophyll A green substance called chlorophyll in plant cells traps the energy from sunlight.

chloroplasts These saclike organelles help the plant make food.

cotyledons The first leaf or leaves of a plant are called cotyledons.

cuticle A waterproof layer called the cuticle covers the epidermis.

cytoplasm This jellylike material surrounds the nucleus of a cell.

epidermis The outer layer of leaf cells is called the epidermis.

fruit A fruit is a protective case for the seeds of a flowering plant.

germination The point at which a seed sprouts its first root and shoot is known as germination.

meristems Plant tissues called meristems contain cells that keep dividing.

mitochondria These organelles help to release energy from food.

nucleus The nucleus is the control center of a cell.

organelle An organelle is part of a cell that does a particular job.

phloem Plant tissue called phloem carries food around a plant.

photosynthesis Plants make food from the energy in sunlight in a process called photosynthesis.

pollen Tiny grains of male cells are called pollen.

pollination Pollen transfer from male parts to female parts of a plant is called pollination.

proteins Substances called proteins are used for growth and repair.

radicle The first root that develops from a seed is called a radicle.

receptacle The receptacle is the swollen tip of a flower stalk.

shoot A shoot is any new plant growth such as from the root.

stomata Tiny holes called stomata can be found in the leaf or green stem of a plant.

transpiration Transpiration is the loss of water through the stomata.

xylem Tubes called xylem carry water and minerals inside plants.

Find Out More

Books

Burnie, David. *Plant*. New York: DK Publishing, 2006.

Johnson, Rebecca L. *Powerful Plant Cells*. Minneapolis, Minnesota: Millbrook Press, 2007.

Snedden, Robert. *Plants & Fungi: Multicelled Life*. 2nd edition. Chicago, IL: Heinemann Library, 2008.

Star, Fleur. *Plant*. New York: DK Publishing, 2005.

Stephens, Nicholas. *Plant Cells and Tissues*. New York: Chelsea House Publishers, 2006.

Stille, Darlene R. *Plant Cells: The Building Blocks of Plants*. Minneapolis, Minnesota: Compass Point Books, 2006.

Websites

http://biology4kids.com/files/plants_main.html
A complete online guide to plants. View the species slideshow, take the plant quiz, and click on the links to find out about the plant world.

http://biology.about.com/od/plantbiology/Plant_Biology.htm
This is another excellent children's guide to plant biology. Take the plant cell quiz to find out exactly how much you know about plant cells.

http://www.enchantedlearning.com/subjects/plants/printouts.shtml
The Enchanted Learning website includes a lot of information about plants and includes many quizzes, printouts, and worksheets.

http://www.mbgnet.net/bioplants
The Missouri Botanical Garden website provides a brief guide to the biology of plants and includes videos and explanations of unusual terms.

Index

Page numbers in **boldface** are illustrations.